Looking at . . . Maiasaura

A Dinosaur from the CRETACEOUS Period

THE NEW
DINOSAUR
COLLECTION

For a free color catalog describing Gareth Stevens' list of high-quality books,
call 1-800-341-3569 (USA) or 1-800-461-9120 (Canada).

Library of Congress Cataloging-in-Publication Data

Vaughan, Jenny.
    Looking at-- Maiasaura/written by Jenny Vaughan; illustrated by Tony Gibbons.
      p. cm. -- (The New dinosaur collection)
    Includes index.
    ISBN 0-8368-1085-6
    1. Maiasaura--Juvenile literature. [1. Maiasaura. 2. Dinosaurs.] I. Gibbons, Tony, ill. II. Title.
III. Series.
QE862.O65V374 1994
  567.9'7--dc20   93-37053

This North American edition first published in 1994 by
Gareth Stevens Publishing
1555 North RiverCenter Drive, Suite 201
Milwaukee, Wisconsin 53212 USA

This U.S. edition © 1994 by Gareth Stevens, Inc. Created with original
© 1993 by Quartz Editorial Services, Premier House, 112 Station Road,
Edgware HA8 7AQ U.K.

Consultant: Dr. David Norman, Director of the Sedgwick Museum of Geology,
University of Cambridge, England.

Additional artwork by Clare Heronneau.

Printed in MEXICO
1 2 3 4 5 6 7 8 9 99 98 97 96 95 94

At this time, Gareth Stevens, Inc., does not use 100 percent recycled paper, although the paper
used in our books does contain about 30 percent recycled fiber. This decision was made after a
careful study of current recycling procedures revealed their dubious environmental benefits.
We will continue to explore recycling options.

Looking at . . . Maiasaura
A Dinosaur from the CRETACEOUS Period

by Jenny Vaughan

Illustrated by Tony Gibbons

THE NEW
DINOSAUR
COLLECTION

Gareth Stevens Publishing
MILWAUKEE

Contents

Introducing
Maiasaura

The nests were made by a dinosaur called **Maiasaura** (MY-A-<u>SAW</u>-RA). The remains of **Maiasaura** and their nests can still be seen today.

Imagine a group of hundreds of giant nests, each the size of a double bed, with enormous dinosaurs standing guard over their eggs and young.

It would be a strange sight. But if you could travel back in time 74 million years to what is now Montana, in the United States, you would have been able to see this nesting colony.

What sort of dinosaur looked after its babies so closely?

Turn the pages that follow, meet **Maiasaura**, and find out what we now know about this fascinating creature.

Maiasaura and its world

Like all dinosaurs, **Maiasaura** died out millions of years ago, so no human has ever seen a live one. If you *could* meet one, you might be frightened — it was almost as long as a bus.

But, in fact, it was probably quite harmless, because it was a plant-eater. It was also a very careful parent. This is why scientists named it *Maiasaura*, which means "good mother lizard."

6

Maiasaura belonged to a group of dinosaurs called **Hadrosaurs** (HAD-ROW-SAWRS). They all lived toward the end of the Cretaceous Period, between 144 and 65 million years ago. In their time, **Hadrosaurs** were the most common dinosaurs of all in the part of the world we now call North America.

The part of America where **Maiasaura** lived so long ago now has hot, dry summers and very cold winters. But in **Maiasaura's** time, the weather was warm all year round, with wet and dry seasons. There were wide rivers and a huge inland sea.

The plants that grew at this time were conifers, ferns, horsetails, and the very first flowering plants — beech, fig, and magnolia trees. There was plenty of food around for **Maiasaura** to eat, so it could have had quite a varied vegetarian diet.

7

Duck-billed dinosaur

The skeletons that scientists have discovered give us a good idea of what **Maiasaura** must have looked like.

The strangest feature of this Cretaceous creature was its face. It looked as if it belonged on a giant duck. All **Hadrosaurs** had faces like this and are often called "duck-billed dinosaurs." But, unlike ducks, they had rows and rows of teeth along the insides of their cheeks.

These teeth were for grinding tough twigs and plants.

Maiasaura had a bony knob between its eyes. It may have used it to head-butt other Maiasaura when fighting over territory or when showing off to a mate.

The skeleton also shows us that Maiasaura had sturdy back legs that were quite a bit longer than its front ones.

Its front feet had small hooves on the ends of some toes. All this means that Maiasaura probably walked around on all four legs at least some of the time, but it could rear up on its back legs if it needed to run.

It may also have reared up to the high branches of trees in order to reach tempting, juicy leaves.

Maiasaura's body was about 30 feet (9 meters) in length. An adult human is not as tall as one of its legs. As you can see, its tail took up a large proportion of its body.

The skeletons of baby Maiasaura have been found in the remains of their nests. Some of these skeletons are much bigger than others. This seems to show that the young stayed in their nests for quite a while after they were born.

Dramatic

Scientists were not always sure that dinosaurs laid eggs. Even when they found evidence, scientists thought the eggs were probably just left somewhere warm to hatch, and that young dinosaurs had to look after themselves.

Then, in 1978, there was an amazing discovery.

Two scientists, Jack Horner and Robert Makela, were in a fossil shop in Montana when they saw the bones of a baby **Hadrosaur**. By asking local people, they finally found the nest that had contained these bones. It was nearby, in some low hills. In the same nest were the remains of several baby dinosaurs!

discovery

But there was something strange about the nest. First, it was full of broken eggshells. This showed that the young had stayed in their nest for a while after hatching, and that they had probably trampled on the shells.

Second, the bones of the babies showed that they had been too young to look for food. But they had teeth that were worn, as if they had been chewing.

The nest belonged to the dinosaur **Maiasaura**. It was Horner and Makela who gave it that name. Over the next few years, they found more and more remains of **Maiasaura** nests and eggs.

Good mothers

Maiasaura nests were made from mud and sand. Each one was bowl-shaped, about 3 to 4 feet (.9 to 1.2 m) deep, and about 6.5 feet (2 m) across.

A mother Maiasaura lined her nest with soft plants and laid about 25 eggs in it. There was always a space left between each egg.

The mothers left this space so the baby Maiasaura could get out of their shells easily when the eggs eventually hatched.

The sun heated the nests by day, and the sand kept the eggs warm at night. Heat from rotting vegetation in the nests also provided warmth.

Some scientists think mother **Maiasaura** may also have curled up around their eggs at night to keep them warm. These mothers took care not to crush their eggs.

The young were only about 14 inches (35 cm) long when they first hatched — that's small enough to fit in your bathroom sink!

But once they hatched, the young grew fast. In two months, they doubled in size.

The baby **Maiasaura** grew fast because they were well fed by their mothers and did not have to use their own energy looking for food. They stayed safe inside the nest while their mothers — and possibly also their fathers — collected food for them.

This meant that if their parents were killed by a meat-eating dinosaur or died in some other way, the young usually died, too.

13

Happy families

The **Maiasaura** nesting areas were on high ground. From there, they could keep a lookout for enemies and be safe from floods.

They all laid their eggs at the same time each year — just before the rainy season began. By the time the young hatched, the rains had come, and there were plenty of fresh plants for them to eat.

Maiasaura parents were kept busy. They each had to find as much as 165 pounds (75 kg) of plants every day for themselves and for their young. That is equal to the weight of a grown human!

Both adult and baby **Maiasaura** had very healthy appetites.

The easiest way for **Maiasaura** to get food for their young was to chew it and swallow it where they found it. They could then regurgitate (spit it out) when they returned to the nests, and the young would eat what their parents brought up. Some birds today feed their young this way.

As the weeks passed, the rainy season ended, and new plants stopped growing.

Plants near the nesting site gradually were eaten, so the parents had to travel farther and farther each day to find food.

But, at last, the young were no longer helpless and grew big enough to leave the nest. So the family could then move to new feeding grounds.

Scientists now believe young **Maiasaura** stayed in their nests until they were nearly three times their birth size. Their mothers, it seems, enjoyed looking after them.

Under attack!

It was a warm morning. The **Maiasaura** colony was quiet. Many of the adults had gone off to search for food, and others were having a nap near their young.

Before long, it was in terrible danger. A swift and fierce meat-eating dinosaur, **Dromaeosaurus** (<u>DROME</u>-EE-OH-<u>SAW</u>-RUS), was nearby.

One bold young **Maiasaura** scrambled out of its nest to explore a little while its mother slept. Its brothers and sisters, meanwhile, peeped over the edge of the nest and watched.

It was creeping through the colony, looking for something to eat for lunch.

Dromaeosaurus was not very tall for a dinosaur. But it had a mouth full of frightening teeth and claws on its hands and feet.

16

The claw on its second toe was very big and could be flicked forward for attacking other dinosaurs.

Slowly, **Dromaeosaurus** crept through the nesting area, trying not to be heard or seen by the dozing dinosaurs. Suddenly, it pounced on the little **Maiasaura**, grasping the terrified baby.

The mother was terrified for her baby. If she had not fallen asleep, she might have stopped it from leaving the safety of the nest and from falling into the **Dromaeosaurus**'s clawed hands.

But **Dromaeosaurus** was much too quick for her, and it had sharper teeth and claws. When face-to-face with it, she was defenseless.

The baby **Maiasaura** squealed in terror. Its brothers and sisters darted back into their nest. Disturbed by the noise, their mother woke up and chased the **Dromaeosaurus**, desperately trying to save her young one.

After only a minute or so, the young **Maiasaura** was dead. The **Dromaeosaurus** now carried it off into some bushes. It would make a delicious meal, and the **Dromaeosaurus** did not want to share it.

17

Migrating dinosaurs

Even when they were not nesting, **Maiasaura** lived in herds, as many plant-eating animals do today.

We know this because scientists have found the bones of tens of thousands of **Hadrosaurs** in the same area. They were probably killed by the poisonous gas and smoke from an erupting volcano.

Such a large number could not have stayed in one place for long before all the plants there would have been eaten. So they must have migrated — traveled from one place to another in search of food.

As soon as their young were old enough to leave their nests, the **Maiasaura** probably moved to an area where there was more rain and more green plants growing.

Hadrosaur tracks also show that large groups of these dinosaurs migrated together across the landscape.

Maiasaura remains show that the young and old traveled together. In one place, scientists found adult bones and the bones of young ones in three different sizes. These were probably one-, two-, and three-year-old **Maiasaura**.

When they reached their new feeding grounds, the **Maiasaura** spread out across the countryside and spent their days grazing. Later in the year, just before the rains, the **Maiasaura** would return to their old nesting sites to lay a new set of eggs and raise another family.

There must also have been extra safety in numbers, so that predators did not attack as often as they otherwise might. Even so, the "good mother" dinosaurs did not always escape danger.

Maiasaura and cousins

Maiasaura (1) belonged to a group of dinosaurs called **Saurolophine** (SAWR-OH-LO-FINE) **Hadrosaurs**. The word *Saurolophine* means "ridged reptile." These dinosaurs had spiky outgrowths on their heads. Some, like **Maiasaura**'s, were very small — no more than a bony lump.

But others had bigger crests. These may have been used to attract mates or to drive off rivals.

Saurolophus (SAWR-OH-LOAF-US) **(2)** first appeared about 74 million years ago in parts of the world we now know as North America and Mongolia. It was bigger than **Maiasaura** and looked similar except for its head. On the top of its skull was a bony ridge that ran backward forming a spike. **Saurolophus** also had flaps of skin around its nose. It may have been able to blow these up and use them to make a honking noise, as elephant seals do today.

2

You can see a young **Tsintaosaurus** (SIN-TOW-SAW-RUS) **(3)** on the opposite page. It lived in a part of the world that is now China, around the same time as **Saurolophus**, but was smaller. Experts once believed that the spike on its head pointed forward, like a unicorn's horn. But we now know this is a mistake and that the horn just formed the roof of its snout.

Prosaurolophus (PRO-SAWR-OH-LOAF-US) **(4)** was just a little smaller than **Maiasaura**. It lived in what we now call Alberta, Canada. Some scientists think that it was not a separate kind of dinosaur at all, but another sort of **Saurolophus**. Its name means "before **Saurolophus**."

Maiasaura data

Maiasaura was a typical **Hadrosaur** — which means it was a plant-eating dinosaur with a long tail. It was not very heavily built. Although it was twice as long as an African elephant, it only weighed half as much as one.

Sturdy limbs
Its front legs, or arms, were long enough to touch the ground when **Maiasaura** walked around on all fours. There were pads under its front toes to help protect the toes from rough ground.

Maiasaura's back legs were longer. They supported the weight of this dinosaur as it made its way through the Cretaceous landscape.

Heavy tail
Maiasaura's tail made up about one-third of its body length. It was thick and flat. **Maiasaura** used it to help balance, especially when it walked on its two back legs. Because of the tail's shape, scientists have also guessed that **Maiasaura** could swim quite well, using the tail to power its way through the water. This would have been useful when escaping from larger, clumsier predators.

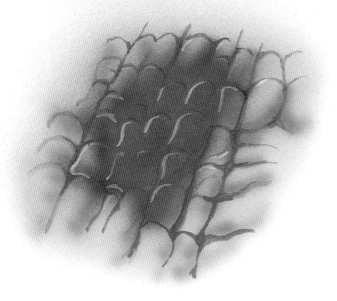

Skin color

Like other dinosaurs, **Maiasaura** had rough skin that may have been a little like an elephant's hide. You can see a portion of its skin above. We do not know for certain what color this was, but it probably matched its background — a deep yellow, green, or brown color.

Maiasaura had no obvious weapons to fight off enemies, such as spikes or tail-clubs, and it was not protected by body armor. So it would have helped to be a color that was hard to see when in its natural surroundings.

Cheek teeth

The front of the mouth of this dinosaur did not contain any teeth, but there were hundreds farther back. These allowed **Maiasaura** to chew its food. (Many earlier dinosaurs could not chew and had to swallow food in lumps.) **Maiasaura** had rows of teeth in the upper and lower parts of its jaw.

Maiasaura used its teeth to grind the plants and twigs it ate. This made the food easier to digest. **Maiasaura**'s teeth rubbed together as it chewed tough leaves. The teeth often wore down, but they always grew back.

GLOSSARY

colony — a group of like animals that live together.

conifers — woody shrubs or trees that bear their seeds in cones.

crest — a growth on top of an animal's head.

fossils — traces or remains of plants and animals found in rock.

hatch — to come out of an egg.

herd — a group of animals that travels together.

hoof (hooves) — a strong covering of horn that protects the feet of certain animals.

migrate — to move from one place or climate to another.

predators — animals that kill other animals for food.

remains — a dead body or corpse.

snout — protruding nose and jaws of an animal.

INDEX